Animal Hospital

FIRST EDITION
Project Editor Naia Bray-Moffatt; **Art Editor** Andrew Burgess; **Photography** John Daniels;
Senior Editor Linda Esposito; **Managing Art Editor** Peter Bailey; **US Editor** Regina Kahney;
Pre-Production Producer Nadine King; **Producer** Sara Hu; **Reading Consultant** Linda Gambrell, PhD

THIS EDITION
Editorial Management by Oriel Square
Produced for DK by WonderLab Group LLC
Jennifer Emmett, Erica Green, Kate Hale, *Founders*

Editors Grace Hill Smith, Libby Romero, Maya Myers, Michaela Weglinski;
Photography Editors Kelley Miller, Annette Kiesow, Nicole DiMella; **Managing Editor** Rachel Houghton;
Designers Project Design Company; **Researcher** Michelle Harris; **Copy Editor** Lori Merritt;
Indexer Connie Binder; **Proofreader** Larry Shea; **Reading Specialist** Dr. Jennifer Albro;
Curriculum Specialist Elaine Larson

Published in the United States by DK Publishing
1745 Broadway, 20th Floor, New York, NY 10019

Copyright © 2023 Dorling Kindersley Limited
DK, a Division of Penguin Random House LLC
23 24 25 26 10 9 8 7 6 5 4 3 2 1
001–334083–July/2023

All rights reserved.

Without limiting the rights under the copyright reserved above, no part of this publication may be reproduced, stored in or introduced into a retrieval system, or transmitted, in any form, or by any means (electronic, mechanical, photocopying, recording, or otherwise), without the prior written permission of the copyright owner.
Published in Great Britain by Dorling Kindersley Limited

A catalog record for this book
is available from the Library of Congress.
HC ISBN: 978-0-7440-7430-7
PB ISBN: 978-0-7440-7431-4

DK books are available at special discounts when purchased in bulk for sales promotions, premiums,
fundraising, or educational use. For details, contact: DK Publishing Special Markets,
1745 Broadway, 20th Floor, New York, NY 10019
SpecialSales@dk.com

Printed and bound in China

The publisher would like to thank the following for their kind permission to reproduce their images:
a=above; c=center; b=below; l=left; r=right; t=top; b/g=background
123RF.com: Blaj Gabriel / justmeyo 10bl; **Dreamstime.com:** Alexsokolov 20–21b, Aspenrock 10, Blanscape 23b. Serhii Bobyk 5, Isselee 29c, Jkha 6b, Monkey Business Images 30–31, Photodeti 3cb, Photographerlondon 4, Photophreak 28b
Cover images: *Front:* **Dreamstime.com:** Photodeti bc, Vectorikart; **Shutterstock.com:** Jan Quist bl;
Back: **Dreamstime.com:** Artinspiring cla

All other images © Dorling Kindersley
For more information see: www.dkimages.com

For the curious
www.dk.com

Level 2

Animal Hospital

Judith Walker Hodge

Contents

6	A Trip to the Vet
12	Time for a Checkup
18	Emergency!
24	A New Home

30 Glossary
31 Index
32 Quiz

A Trip to the Vet

One day, Ana and Felix were playing near their house when they heard a strange noise. They went to see what it was.

"It's a duck," said Felix. "Its wing looks hurt."

"We shouldn't move it," said Ana. "Let's get Dad."

quack quack

Dad got a cardboard box.

He put the duck gently into the box.

Then, the family drove to the animal hospital.

Mallard Ducks

The duck in this story is a female mallard duck. Male mallard ducks are more colorful. They have green heads and yellow beaks.

"Hello," said the vet. "I'm Dr. Lee. What have we got here?"

She took the duck out of the box and looked at it carefully.

Bird Wings

Bird wings are fragile. They are mostly hollow, which means they are light. This makes it easier for birds to fly.

"She's hurt her wing," said the vet. "But luckily it isn't broken."

Dr. Lee strapped the wing to the bird's body with a bandage.

"It will take about three weeks to heal," she told the children.

Andrew, one of the nurses, took the duck to a special area out back.

"All the birds are kept here," he said.

Vet Training

It takes five years to train to become a vet. Vets need to know how to care for lots of different animals.

The nurse put some pellets and fresh water on the ground next to the duck.

"Can we come and visit her?" Felix asked.

"Sure," said the nurse. "Come back next week."

"Thanks!" said the children. They rushed inside to tell their parents.

Time for a Checkup

Ana's friend Alice was in the waiting room. She was holding a rabbit. On the floor beside her was a basket.

"Look what I've got!" said Alice. Ana opened the basket and out jumped five kittens!

"We've brought them for a checkup," said Alice's mom. "Can you help carry the kittens into the vet's room?"

"Hello again," said the vet as the children came in.

"They're helping Alice," said Alice's mom with a smile.

The vet listened to each kitten's heart and lungs with her stethoscope.

She looked into their eyes and ears and checked their fur for fleas.

Then, she gave each kitten a shot to protect it against cat flu and other illnesses.

Caring for Cats

Cats need their fur checked often for fleas. They need to be checked for worms, too.

Next, it was the rabbit's turn.

"He's not eating," Alice told the vet.

Dr. Lee looked inside the rabbit's mouth.

"I think I know what the problem is," she said.

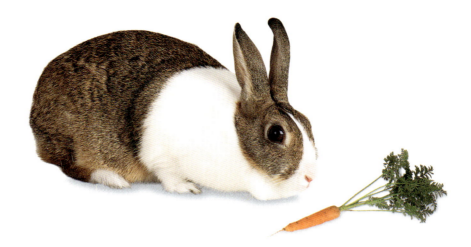

"His teeth are too long—no wonder he can't chew his carrots!"

The vet clipped the teeth with a pair of special scissors.

"It doesn't hurt him, I promise," she told the children.

Rabbit Teeth

A rabbit's teeth never stop growing. That's because in the wild they eat rough plant stems, which wear their teeth down.

Emergency!

quack quack

The next week, Ana and Felix went back to the hospital. The duck was now waddling around the yard, quacking happily.

"She can't swim yet because of the bandage," Dr. Lee told the children.

"Her webbed feet will crack if they get too dry. Would you like to help sponge them?"

"Yes!" said the children.

But just then, a siren went off.

ring   *ring*   *ring*

The children followed Dr. Lee to the animal ambulance.

"What have we got?" she asked the nurse.

"A dog has been hit by a car," said the nurse. "His front leg looks broken."

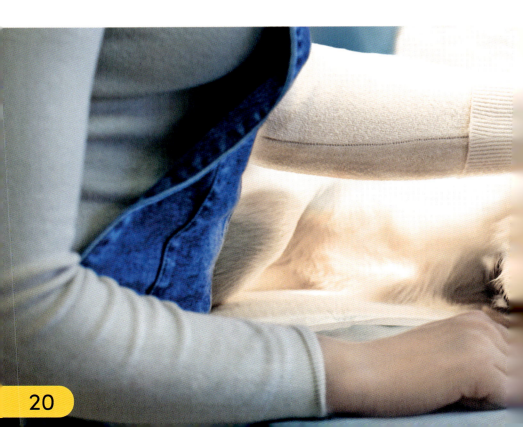

X-rays

These are special photographs taken by invisible rays. The rays pass through the body and show the bones.

"We'll need to take some X-rays right away," said the vet. "Let's get him inside."

Dr. Lee showed the children the X-rays.

"Look," she pointed. "Can you see the broken bone?"

Ana and Felix nodded.

"I'll have to operate to fix it. You two wait outside."

Dr. Lee made sure everything was clean. She put on a gown and a special mask. Then, she scrubbed her hands.

"The dog will be fine," said the vet after the operation.

A New Home

Two weeks later, Ana and Felix went back to visit the duck.

They watched Dr. Lee take off the bandage and check the duck's wing.

"She's ready to go home," said the vet. "All we have to do is find her one."

Just then Andrew came in.

"A corn snake is missing," he told the vet.

"Can I help look for it?" asked Felix. "I love snakes."

"No, no," said Dr. Lee. "Corn snakes are harmless. I'm sure it will turn up."

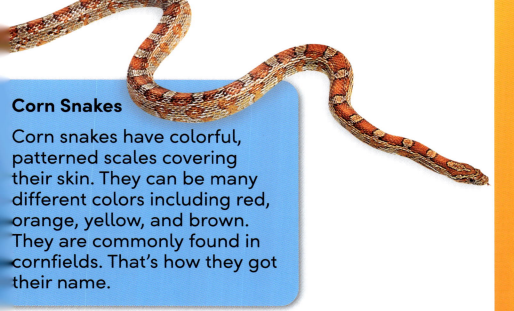

Corn Snakes

Corn snakes have colorful, patterned scales covering their skin. They can be many different colors including red, orange, yellow, and brown. They are commonly found in cornfields. That's how they got their name.

The next day, Dr. Lee phoned the children's home.

"I've found a place for the duck," she told their mother, "at a farm with a pond. Can the children come with me?"

"Of course!" said Mom.

At the farm, the vet went to the barn to look at a horse with an infected hoof.

The children watched the vet clean the horse's foot. Then, she gave the animal a shot to fight the infection.

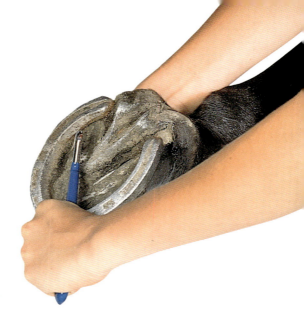

"I'm almost done here," she said to the children.

"Why don't you show the duck her new home on the pond?"

Horseshoes

Horses wear metal shoes to protect their feet. The job of reshoeing horses is done by a farrier. Shoes last four to eight weeks.

27

Lots of ducks were swimming in the farm pond.

Ana took the duck out of her box. She didn't move.

"Go on," Ana whispered.

The duck spread her wings, stepped into the pond, and swam off with the other ducks.

Dr. Lee was putting her instruments away in her bag.

"There's something moving in there!" cried Felix.

Dr. Lee looked inside and laughed.

"You found the snake after all!" said the vet.

Glossary

Bandage
A strip of cloth used to protect or cover a wound

Checkup
An examination done by a doctor

Farrier
Someone who puts metal horseshoes on horses

Fleas
Tiny wingless insects that can jump far and suck the blood of animals

Fragile
Easily broken

Hoof
A hard, tough covering on the feet of animals such as horses and pigs

Infected
Containing disease or germs

Operation
A surgery or medical procedure done by a doctor to repair damage

Stethoscope
An instrument used to hear sounds inside the body, such as a heartbeat

Vet
A short word for veterinarian; a doctor who cares for animals

Waddling
Walking with short steps while rocking from side to side

X-ray
A special photograph that shows the bones inside a body

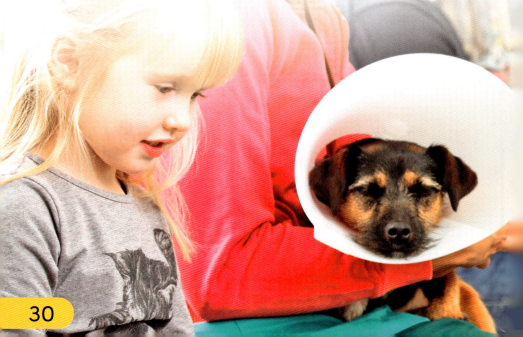

Index

index text   20

index subhead
   index sub entry   33

index text   45

Quiz

Answer the questions to see what you have learned. Check your answers in the key below.

1. What kind of animal did Ana and Felix find and help?

2. What kind of doctor treated the animal?

3. Why did the kittens get shots?

4. What was wrong with the rabbit's teeth and why did this happen?

5. What does an X-ray do?

1. Mallard duck 2. A veterinarian 3. To protect against cat flu and other illnesses 4. They were too long because a rabbit's teeth never stop growing 5. It shows the bones inside a body